THE GREATEST DOT TO DOT!

DAVID KALVITIS

MONKEYING AROUND

Book 6

By David Kalvitis

Fourth Edition

monkeying around &

www.monkeyingaround.com

Rochester, New York

Book 6

By David Kalvitis

Fourth Edition

Copyright © 2008 by David R. Kalvitis
First Printing 2008, Reprinted 2008, 2009, 2010
Printed in the United States of America

Monkeying Around
PO Box 10131
Rochester, New York 14610 USA
585-256-2660
800-553-4300
Fax: 585-442-2965
info@monkeyingaround.com
www.monkeyingaround.com

Rochester, **New York**

Rules & Regulations?

There are only two basic rules to keep in mind...

1. Try to use a relatively straight line when connecting dots for the most accurate picture.

2. Follow the numbers in numerical order for the intended image to become visible.

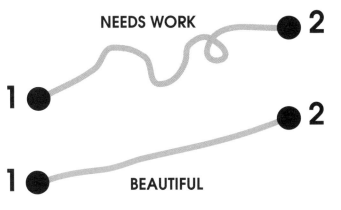

NEEDS WORK

BEAUTIFUL

Long Distances!

When connecting dots that seem a vast distance apart, try this helpful hint.

1. Put your writing implement on the starting dot.

2. Focus your eyes on the "target" dot to which you are heading.

3. Keeping your eyes fixed on the "target" dot, drag your pen along the paper until you reach the dot. You should end up with a fairly straight line.

Pen Size?

Just a suggestion...

Using a fairly thick pen or marker will allow the final image to triumphantly emerge from a stormy sea of dots and numbers.

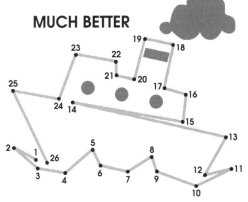

MUCH BETTER

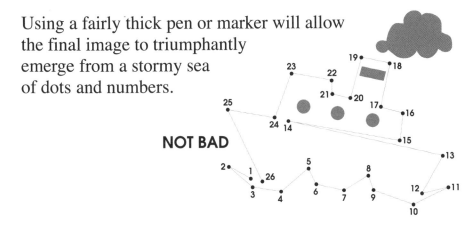

NOT BAD

Stars

Stop at each star (★), then skip to the next number and start your line again.

End ★ 184

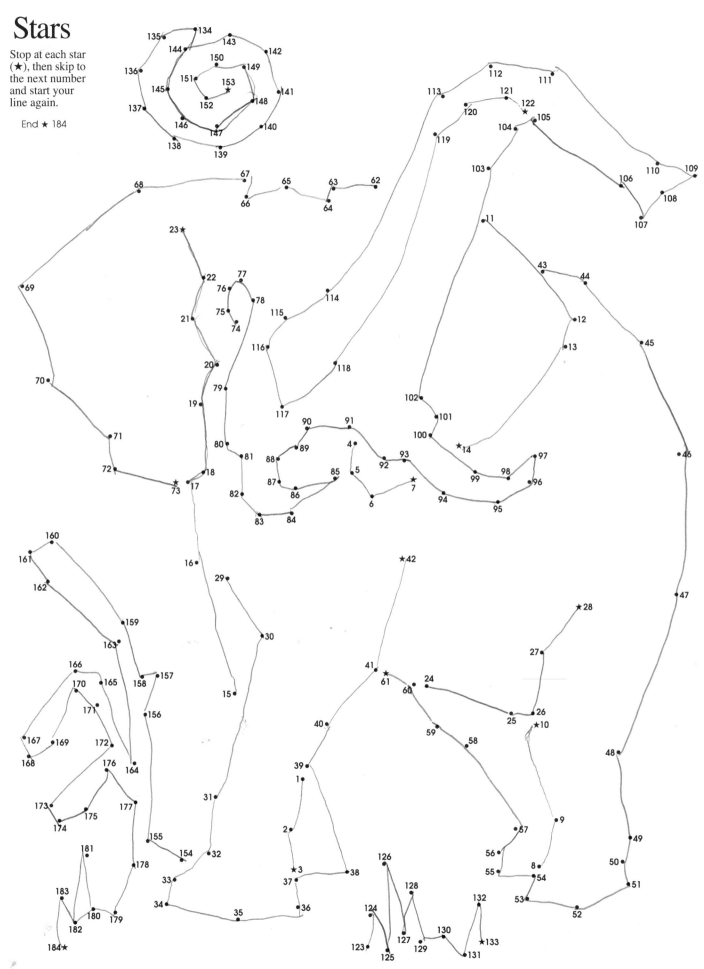

© 2008 Monkeying Around

No Dots!

Connect Numbers:

1 – 280

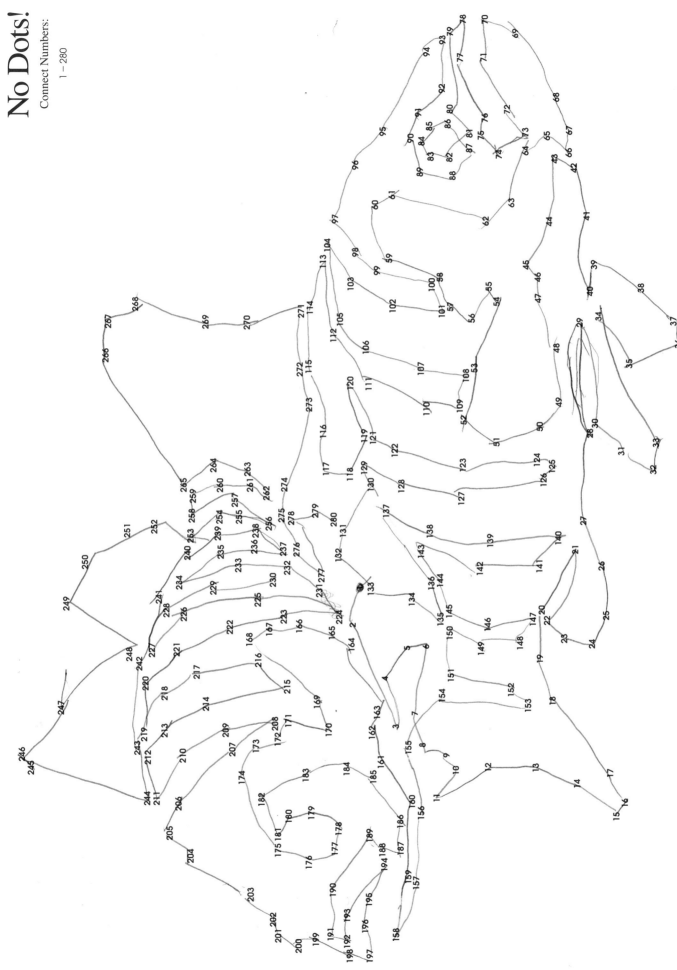

© 2008 Monkeying Around

Tip: Aim for the middle of each number.

Sets

Stop your line after completing each set, then skip to the next set and start your line again.

- ❑ ● 1 thru 36
- ❑ ▲ 37 thru 40
- ❑ ■ 41 thru 47
- ❑ ♦ 48 thru 84
- ❑ ● 85 thru 111
- ❑ ▲ 112 thru 144
- ❑ ■ 145 thru 299

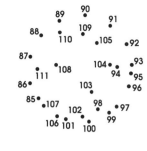

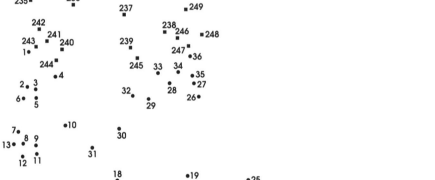

Connect Dots:
- 1 – 272
- A1 – A4
- B1 – B10
- C1 – C14

© 2008 Monkeying Around

7

Sets

Stop your line after
completing each
set, then skip to the
next set and start
your line again.

- ● 1 thru 2
- ▲ 3 thru 4
- ■ 5 thru 6
- ◆ 7 thru 8
- ● 9 thru 10
- ▲ 11 thru 13
- ■ 14 thru 17
- ◆ 18 thru 24
- ● 25 thru 48
- ▲ 49 thru 68
- ■ 69 thru 95
- ◆ 96 thru 258

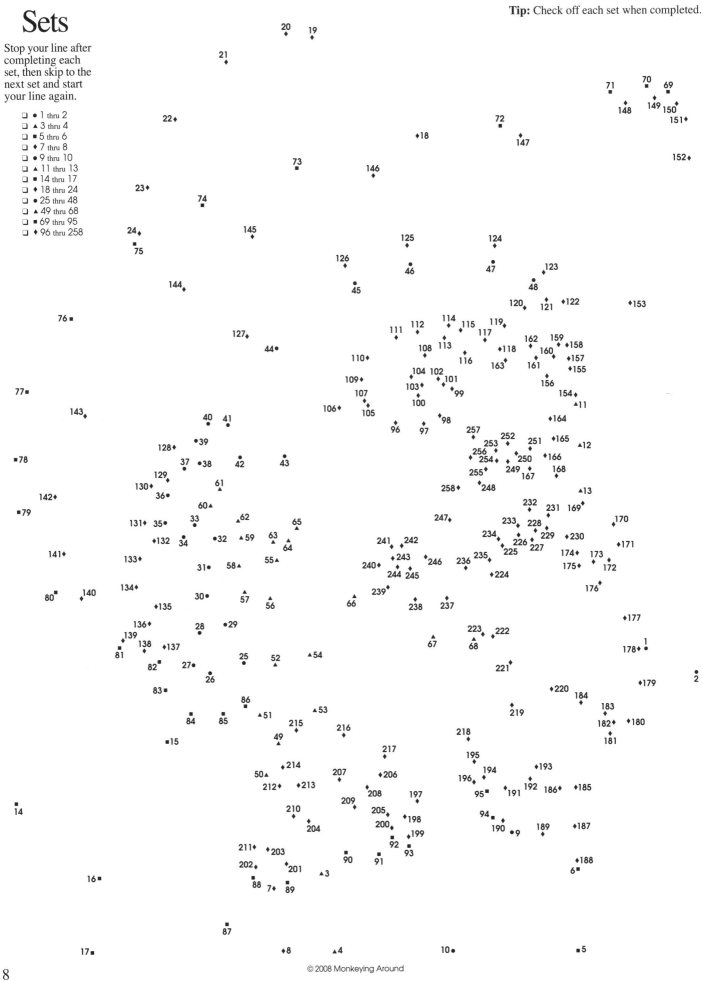

8

© 2008 Monkeying Around

Stars

Stop at each star
(★), then skip to
the next number
and start your
line again.

End ★ 492

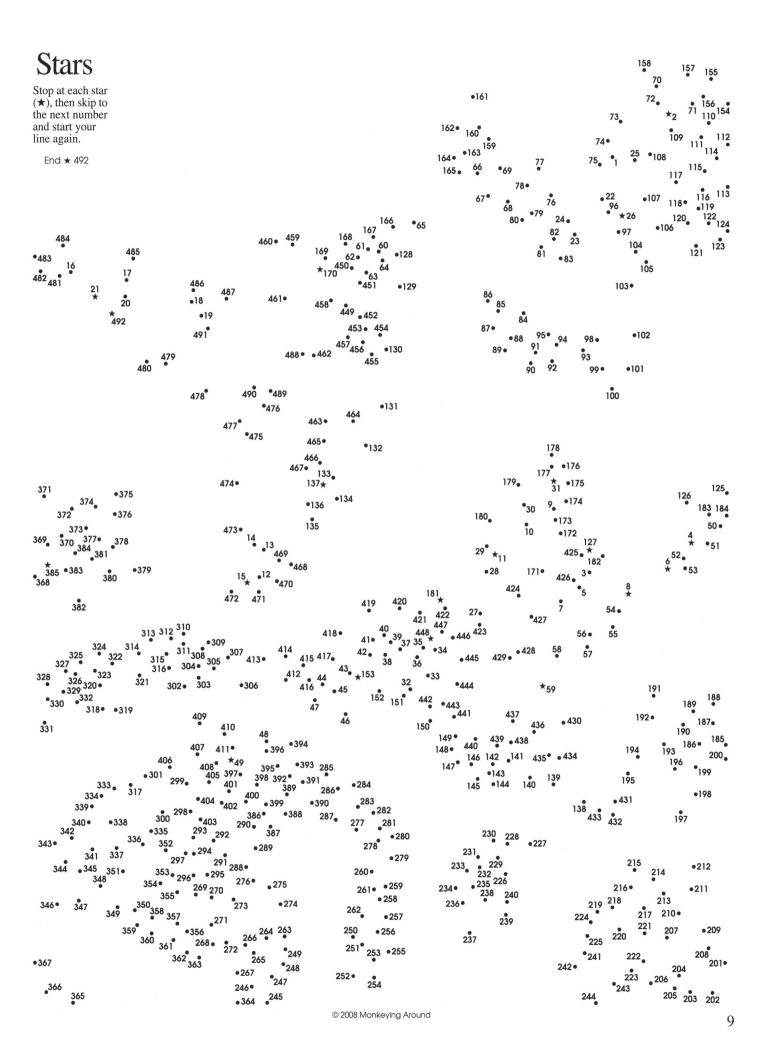

9

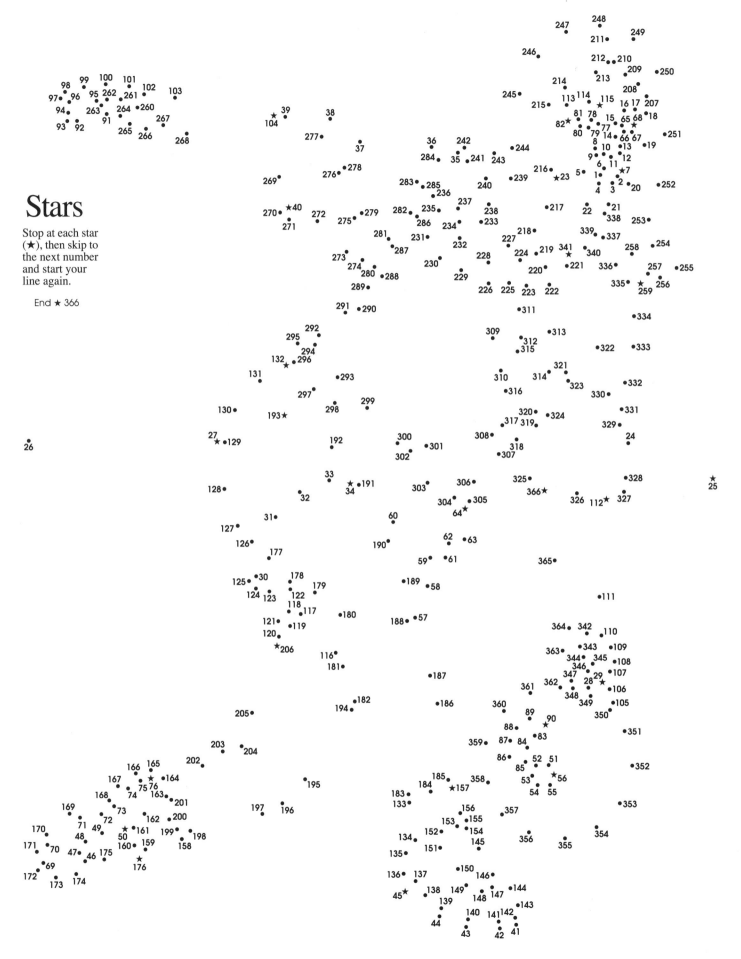

Stars

Stop at each star
(★), then skip to
the next number
and start your
line again.

End ★ 366

Symbols

After connecting a set of symbols, skip to another set of symbols and start your line again. Repeat for each set of symbols.

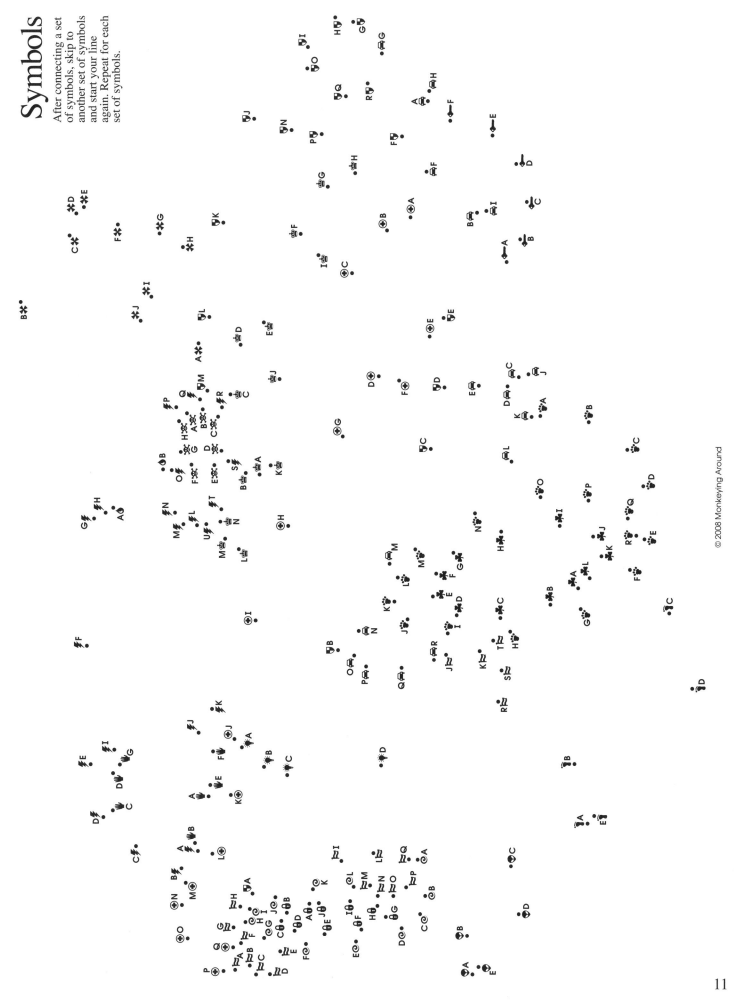

11

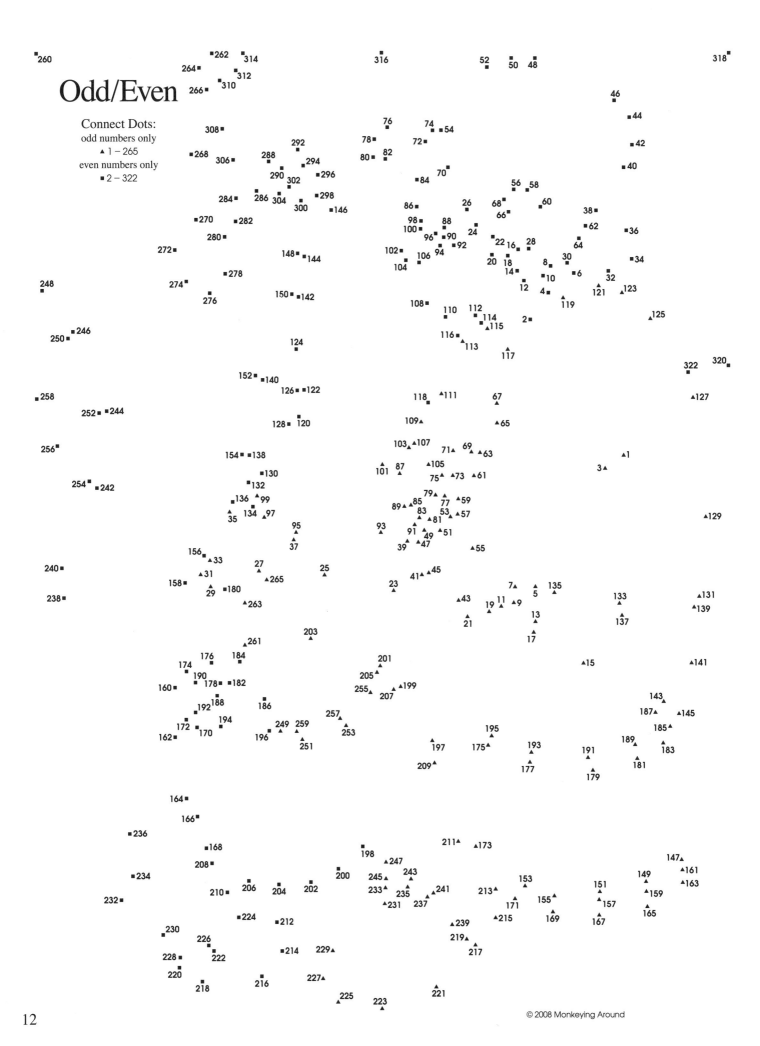

Odd/Even

Connect Dots:
odd numbers only
▲ 1 – 265
even numbers only
■ 2 – 322

Connect Dots:

• 1 – 496

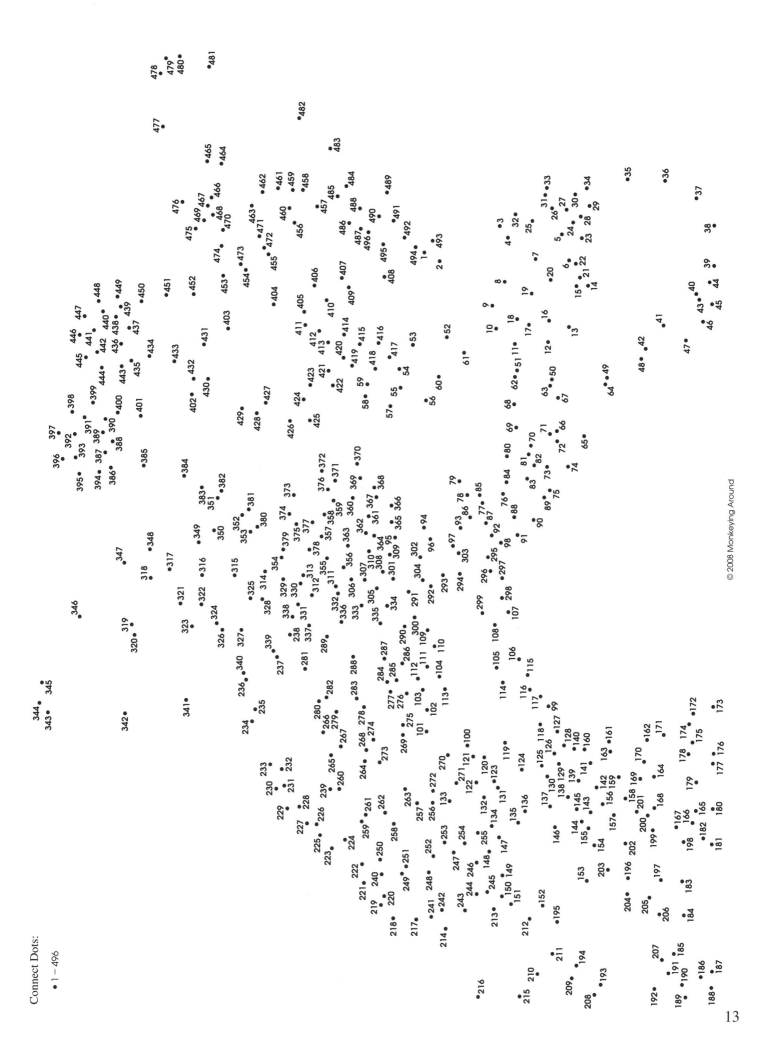

13

Stars

Stop at each star (★), then skip to the next number and start your line again.

End ★ 358

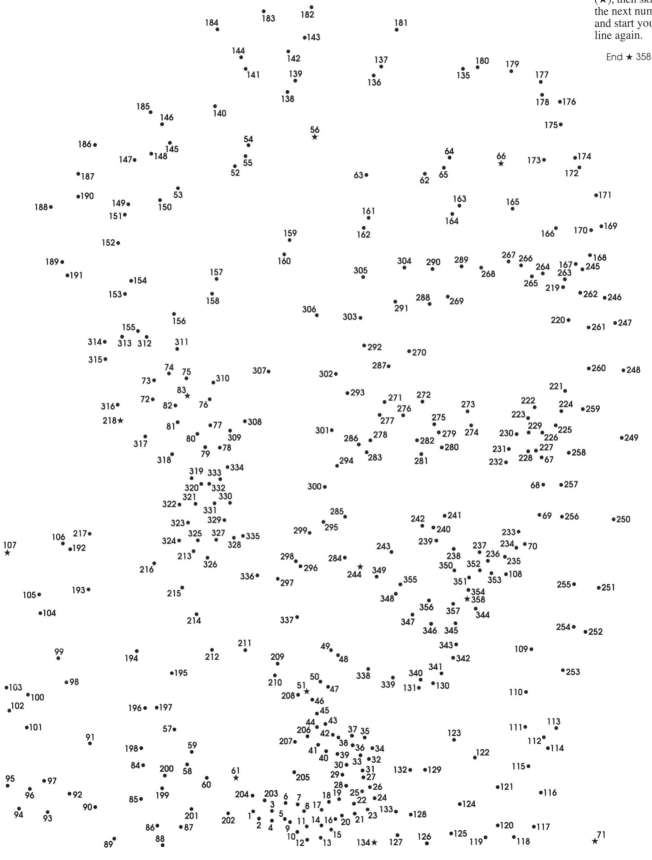

Crazy Dots

Connect Dots:

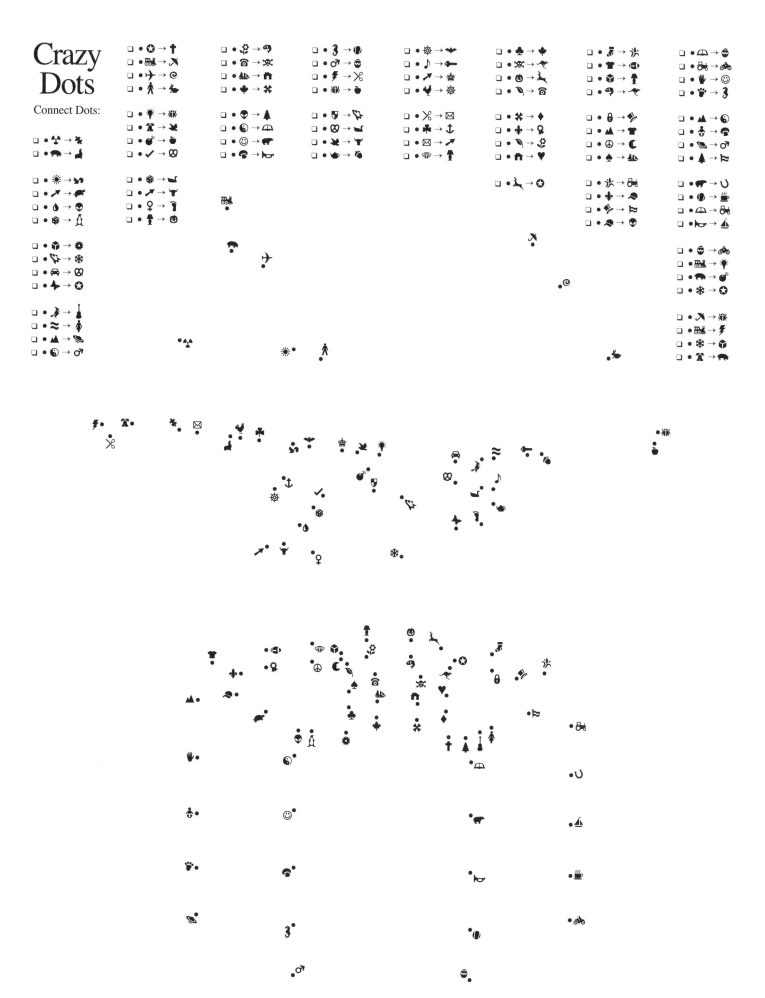

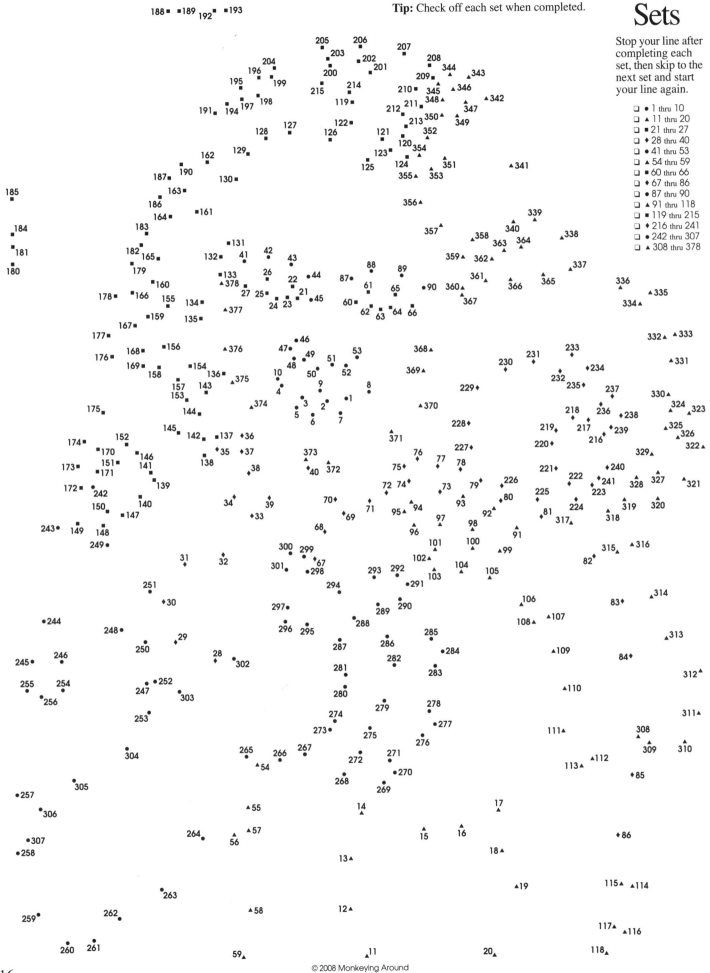

Sets

Stop your line after completing each set, then skip to the next set and start your line again.

- ● 1 thru 10
- ▲ 11 thru 20
- ■ 21 thru 27
- ♦ 28 thru 40
- ● 41 thru 53
- ▲ 54 thru 59
- ■ 60 thru 66
- ♦ 67 thru 86
- ● 87 thru 90
- ▲ 91 thru 118
- ■ 119 thru 215
- ♦ 216 thru 241
- ● 242 thru 307
- ▲ 308 thru 378

Stars

Stop at each star
(★), then skip to
the next number
and start your
line again.

End ★ 459

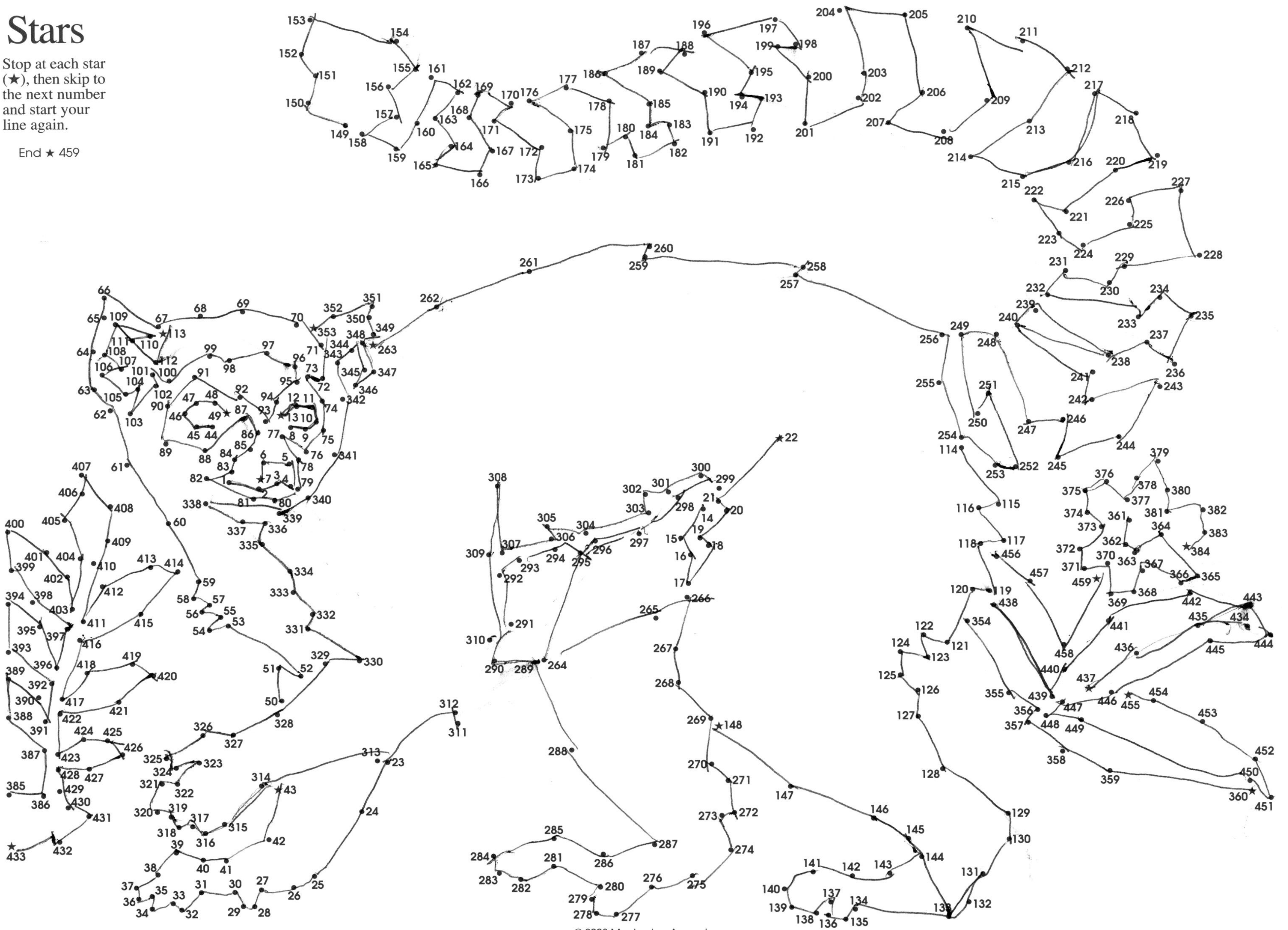

© 2008 Monkeying Around

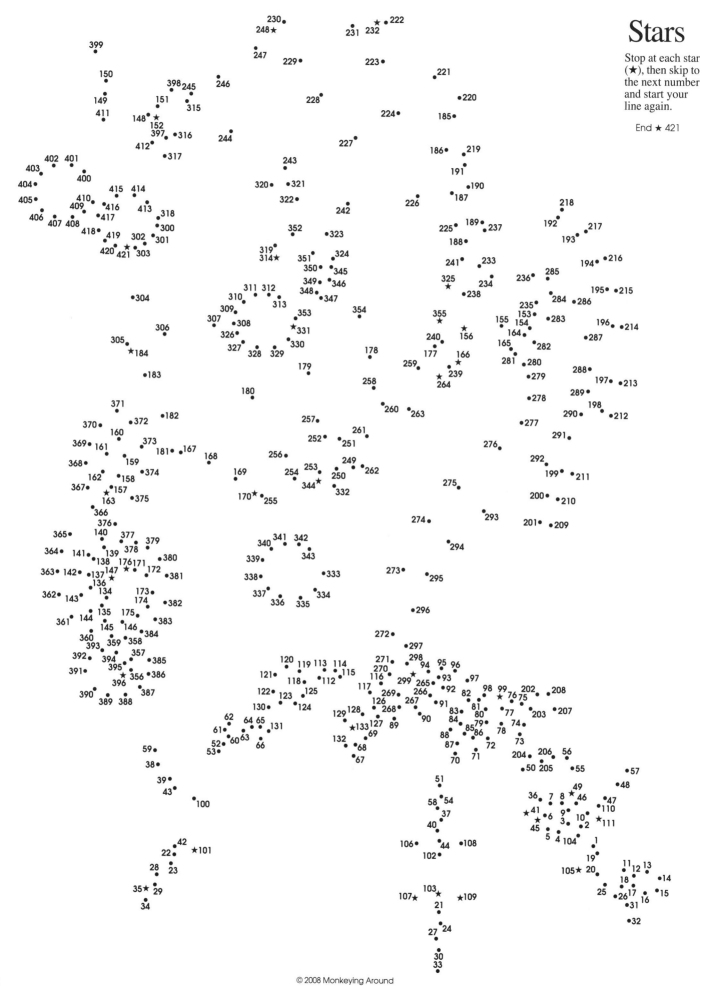

Stars

Stop at each star (★), then skip to the next number and start your line again.

End ★ 421

Stars

Stop at each star (★), then skip to the next number and start your line again.

End ★ 470

After connecting the "A"
set, skip to the "B" set
and start your line again.
Repeat for "C" set, and
so on.

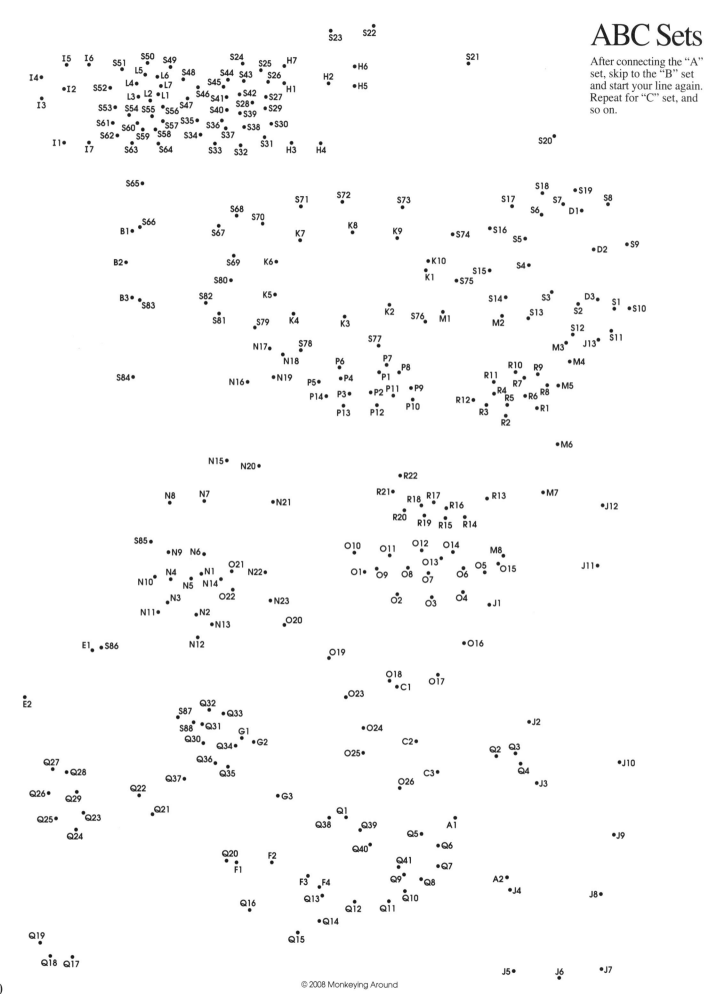

Field of Dots

Circling the "target" dots helps.
Passing thru other dots is okay.

Connect Coordinates:

□	●
H1 → I1	M7 → L9
G3 → J3	O5 → N6
L10 → M10	Q9 → P10
S10 → T10	K15 → J16
M11 → N11	Q10 → P11
N9 → O9	L15 → K16
R12 → S12	S9 → P10
G13 → H13	E18 → D22
U16 → V16	P10 → N11
L18 → O18	M15 → L16
G19 → H19	S10 → R11
W20 → X20	M16 → L17
V21 → Y21	R13 → Q14
R22 → T22	T15 → P19
W22 → Z22	J24 → H26
N23 → O23	P5 → O6
U23 → Z23	V15 → U16
F26 → H26	J27 → H28
G28 → H28	V16 → U17
B23 → B24	L25 → J27
C4 → C5	V21 → T22
D22 → D24	U23 → N25
D26 → D28	W20 → U21
E11 → E12	W22 → M24
E15 → E16	P21 → O23
F13 → F14	O6 → N8
I10 → I12	D24 → F26
I14 → I16	E27 → G28
J22 → J24	B24 → D24
K5 → K6	B23 → D24
K9 → K10	I21 → J22
K16 → K17	E16 → G19
L16 → L17	M22 → N23
L21 → L25	H19 → I21
M4 → M7	K19 → M21
M19 → M20	E12 → F13
M21 → M22	M20 → N22
N8 → N9	I16 → K18
P11 → P13	O18 → P19
P19 → P21	H13 → I14
Q4 → Q9	S20 → U21
S10 → S14	M15 → O16
T11 → T12	K10 → L11
V14 → V15	P13 → Q14
W1 → W18	J10 → K11
E2 → H1	U17 → X20
G3 → C5	L10 → M11
E2 → C4	Q10 → R11
G9 → E11	R13 → T15
K6 → I8	T12 → V14
K9 → I10	K9 → P10
I8 → G9	L2 → M4
Q4 → O5	S9 → T10
M8 → L9	J3 → K5
I12 → G13	I1 → L2
N6 → M8	Y21 → Z22
F14 → E15	

© 2008 Monkeying Around

21

2 Pages

Puzzle crosses over both pages. Stop at each star (★), skip to the next number and start your line again.

End ★ 919

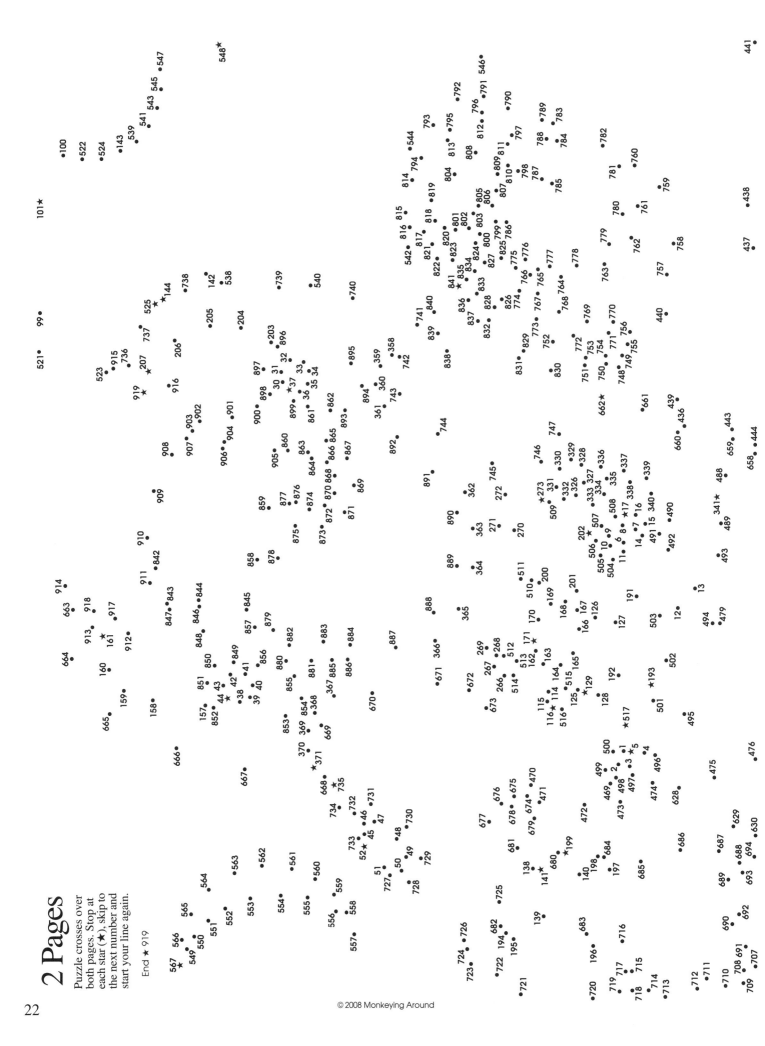

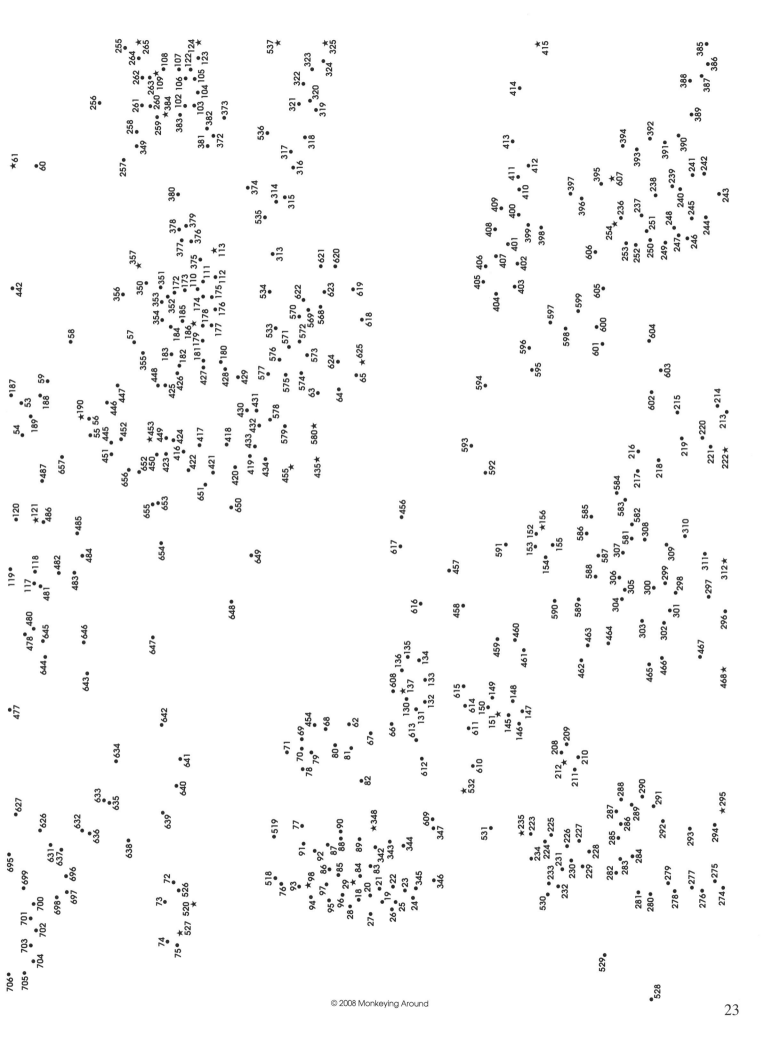

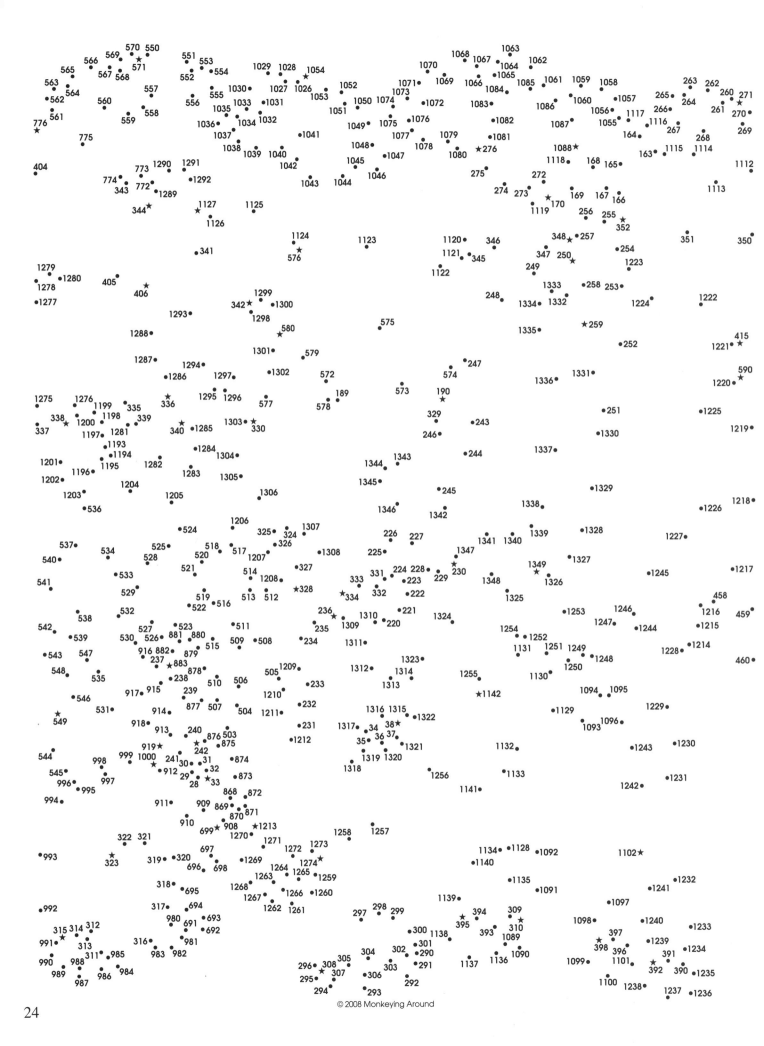

© 2008 Monkeying Around

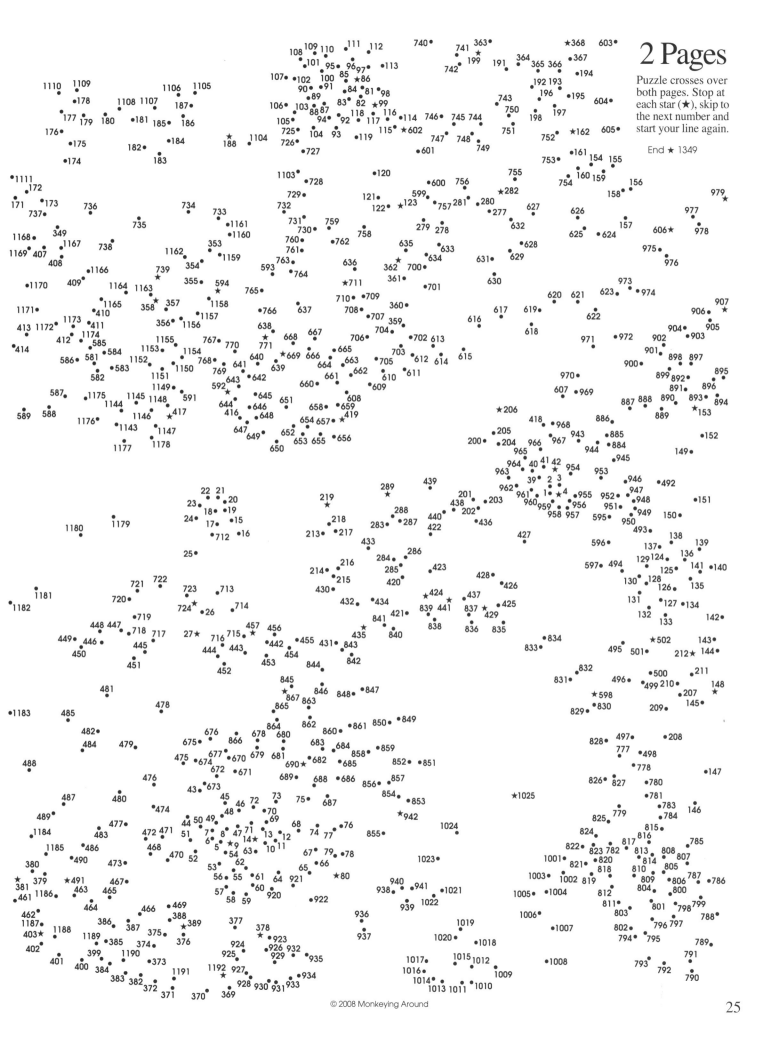

2 Pages

Puzzle crosses over both pages. Stop at each star (★), skip to the next number and start your line again.

End ★ 1349

2 Pages

Puzzle crosses over both pages. Stop at each star (★), skip to the next number and start your line again.

End ★ 693

Warning: Very long lines. **Tip:** Use a ruler.

26

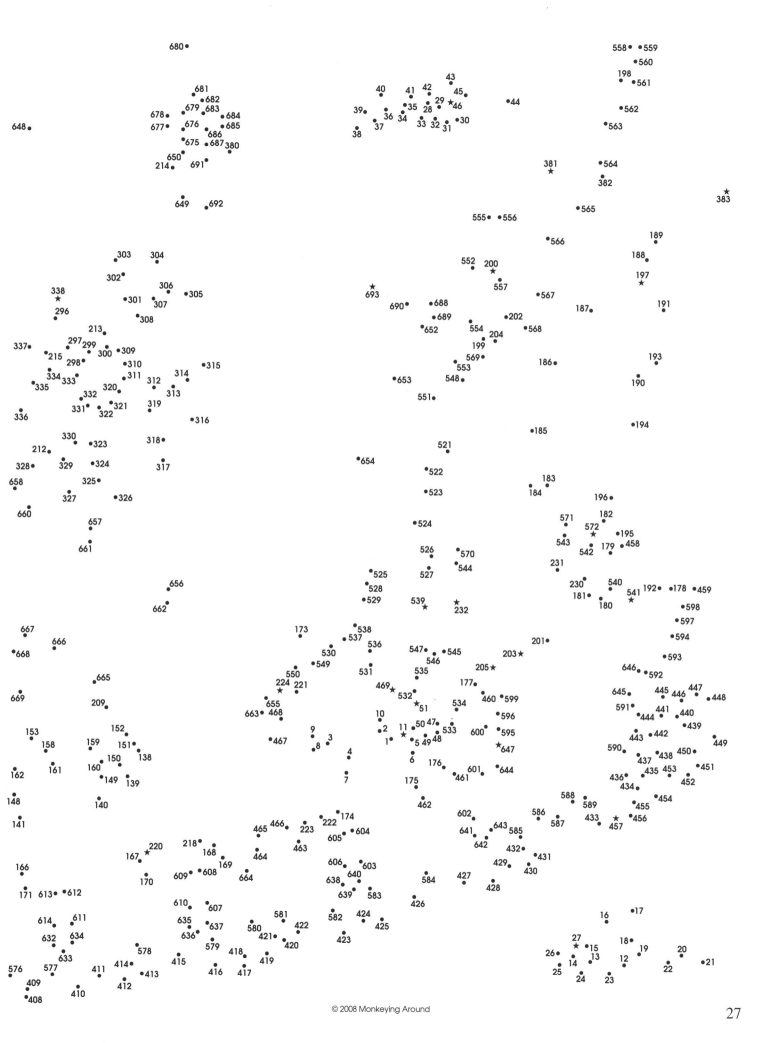

★ ➤ SW x 4 ➤ S x 2 ➤ SW x 2 ➤ S x 4 ➤ SE ➤ S x 4 ➤ SW ➤ S x 5 ➤ SW ➤ S ➤ SW x 3 ➤ S ➤ E ➤ SE ➤ E ➤ SE ➤ E x 2 ➤ NE = A
A ➤ E ➤ NE x 2 ➤ N ➤ NE x 2 ➤ N x 3 ➤ W ➤ NW x 3 ➤ N x 2 ➤ NE ➤ N ➤ NW x 3 ➤ N x 3 ➤ SE ➤ S x 2 ➤ SE x 3 ➤ N x 2 ➤ NE ➤ NW x 5 = B
B ➤ NE x 2 ➤ NW ➤ W ➤ S ➤ NW ➤ N ➤ NE x 3 ➤ E x 3 ➤ SE x 3 ➤ SW ➤ S ➤ NW x 2 ➤ W x 2 ➤ SE x 2 ➤ E ➤ SE ➤ SW x 3 ➤ SE x 8 = C
C ➤ E ➤ SW x 2 ➤ NW x 6 ➤ SW ➤ S ➤ SW x 2 ➤ S ➤ SW ➤ S ➤ SE x 3 ➤ E x 4 ➤ NE ➤ N ➤ NE ➤ N x 2 ➤ NE x 3 ➤ E ➤ SE = D
D ➤ S x 2 ➤ SW x 3 ➤ W ➤ SW ➤ SE ➤ E x 2 ➤ NE x 3 ➤ N x 4 ➤ SE ➤ S x 4 ➤ SW ➤ S x 2 ➤ SE ➤ S x 2 ➤ SE x 2 ➤ S ➤ SW ➤ W x 3 = E
E ➤ NW ➤ W x 5 ➤ SE ➤ E x 2 ➤ SE ➤ E ➤ SE ➤ E x 4 ➤ NE ➤ SE ➤ E x 2 ➤ NE x 4 ➤ E ➤ NE x 2 ➤ N x 5 ➤ NW x 3 = F
F ➤ N x 4 ➤ NW x 2 ➤ N x 4 ➤ NW x 4 ➤ W ➤ N ➤ NW x 3 ➤ N ➤ NW x 6 ➤ W ➤ SW ➤ W x 6 ➤ W ➤ SW x 6 ➤ S ➤ SW x 2 ➤ N ➤ NW x 6 ➤ W ➤ SW = G
G ➤ E ➤ SE x 2 ➤ SW ➤ W ➤ S x 2 ➤ SE x 2 ➤ E ➤ NE ➤ NW ➤ W ➤ NW ➤ N ➤ E ➤ SE x 5 ➤ SW ➤ S x 4 ➤ SW ➤ S x 4 = H
H ➤ NE x 2 ➤ N x 2 ➤ NE ➤ N x 4 ➤ NE ➤ N ➤ NE x 3 ➤ S x 8 ➤ SW x 2 ➤ S ➤ SW x 5 ➤ NW ➤ N x 5 ➤ SW ➤ NW x 4 ➤ N ➤ NW x 3 ➤ N = I
I ➤ NW ➤ N x 4 ➤ NE x 2 ➤ N ➤ NE ➤ E x 2 ➤ NE ➤ NW ➤ W x 6 ➤ SW ➤ W ➤ SW x 4 ➤ S ➤ SW x 2 ➤ S x 6 ➤ NE ➤ N x 4 ➤ NE x 2 = J
J ➤ SE ➤ S ➤ SW ➤ NW ➤ S X 2 ➤ NE X 4 ➤ N X 4 ➤ NW = K

Compass

Start at the star (★), and follow the compass directions to the next dot in the sequence. Each line of instructions will lead you to a letter, to help keep you on track.

Stars

Stop at each star (★), then skip to the next number and start your line again.

End ★ 601

29

Alpha Dots

Start with the word "act", and connect all the words in alphabetical order, ending with the word "zoo".

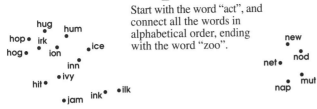

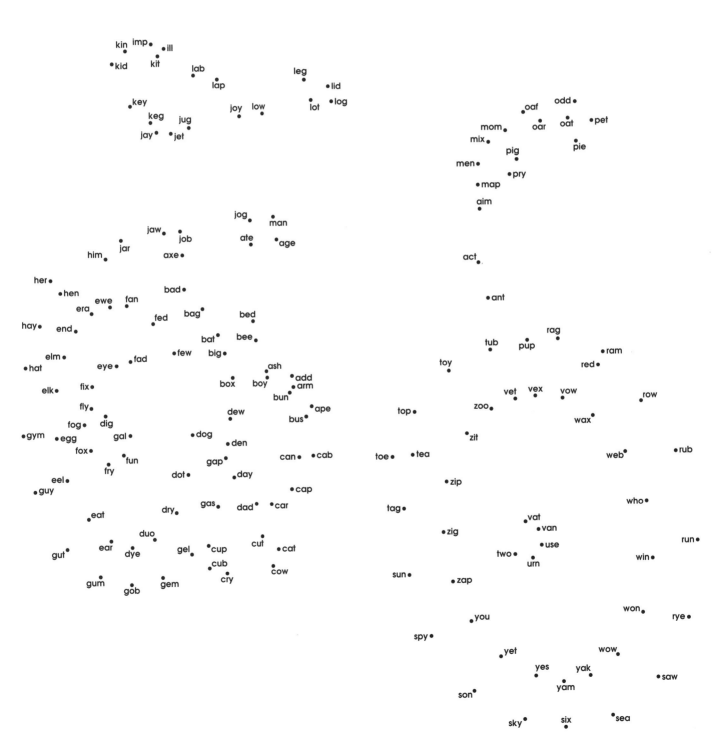

© 2008 Monkeying Around

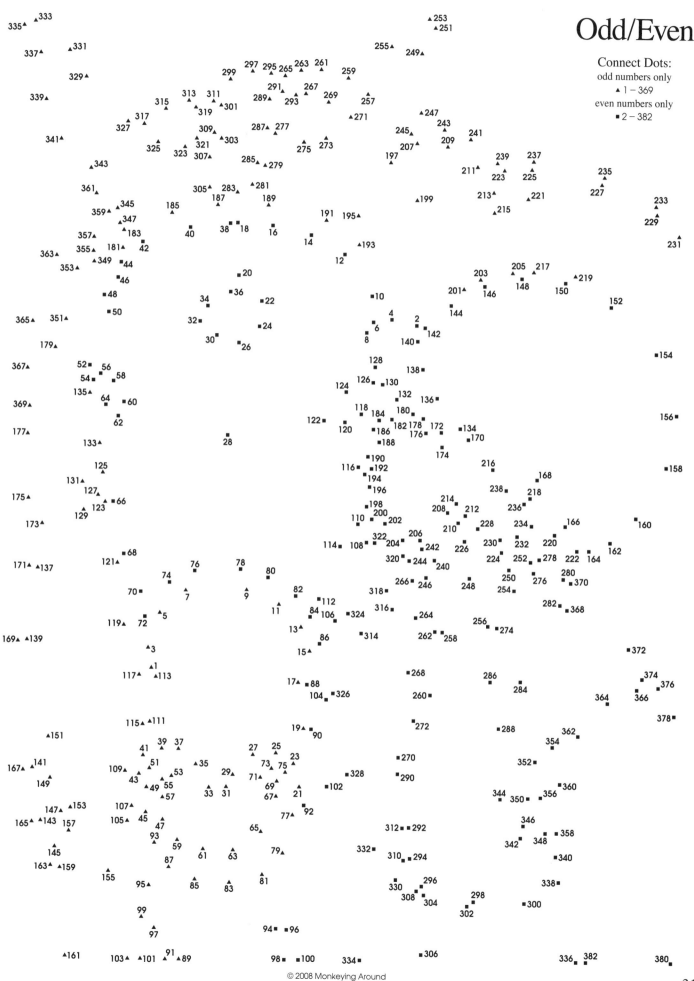

Odd/Even

Connect Dots:
odd numbers only
▲ 1 − 369
even numbers only
■ 2 − 382

© 2008 Monkeying Around

31

Arrows

Start at circled arrow. Move pen in the direction circled arrow points, to the middle of the next arrow. Follow the direction each arrow points. End at circled dot.

Sets

Stop your line after completing each set, then skip to the next set and start your line again.

Tip: Check off each set when completed.

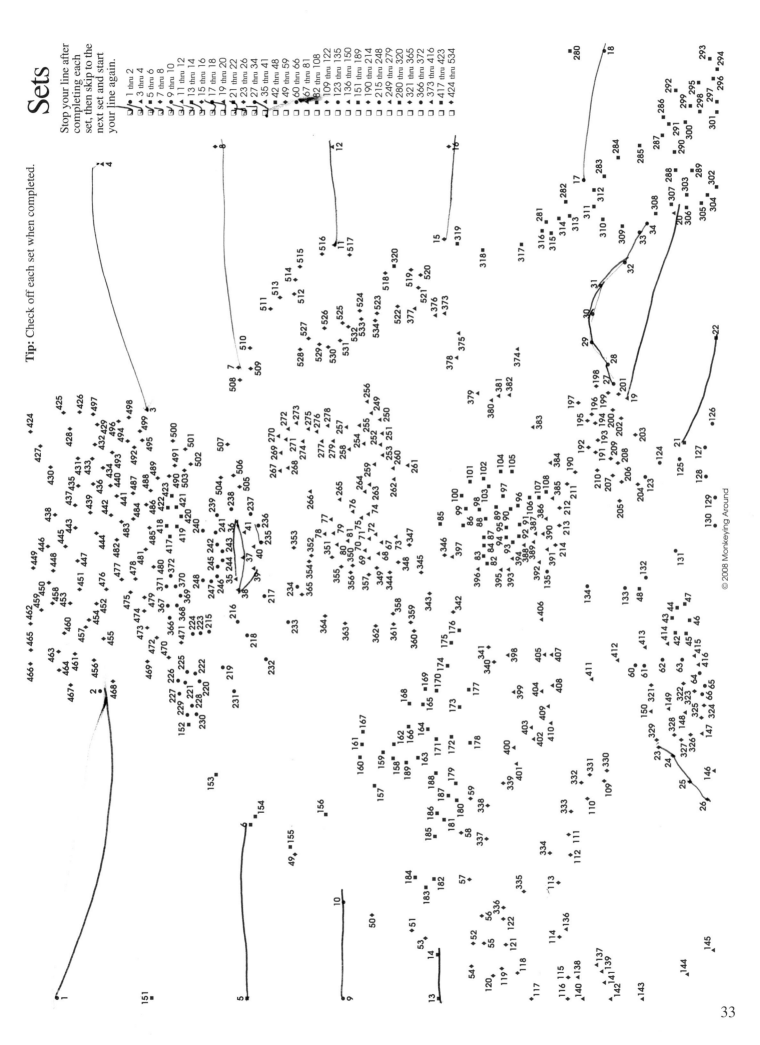

© 2008 Monkeying Around

33

After connecting the "A" set, skip to the "B" set and start your line again. Repeat for "C" set, and so on.

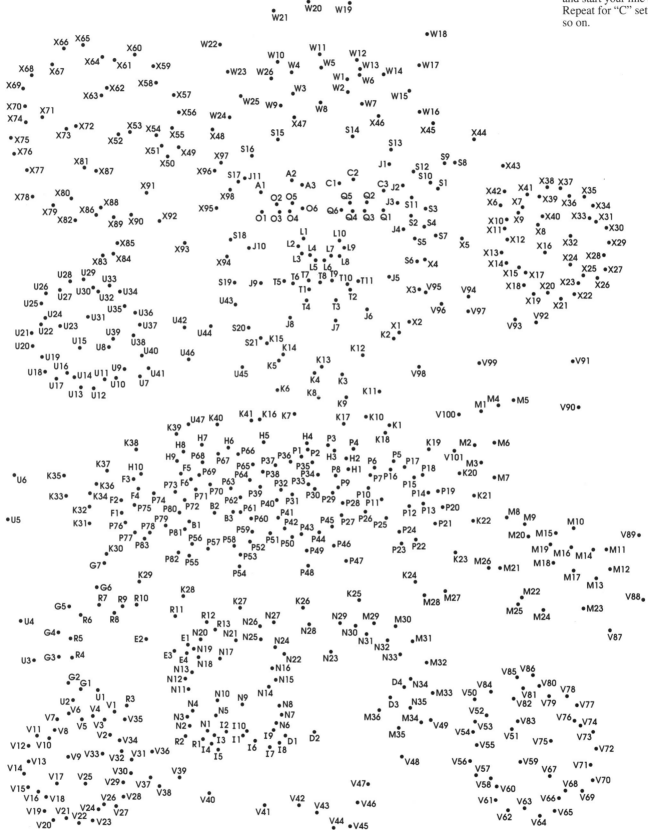

Field of Dots

Circling the "target" dots helps.
Passing thru other dots is okay.

Connect Coordinates:

☐ • K 6 → N 6	☐ • V 9 → U 10
☐ • L 7 → M 7	☐ • Q 20 → P 22
☐ • O 7 → Q 7	☐ • U 15 → T 16
☐ • G 8 → H 8	☐ • Y 14 → W 16
☐ • D 9 → E 9	☐ • U 16 → Q 20
☐ • N 9 → U 9	☐ • K 24 → P 22
☐ • V 9 → X 9	☐ • W 14 → V 15
☐ • B 10 → D 10	☐ • V 9 → X 9
☐ • T 10 → V 10	☐ • O 13 → P 12
☐ • T 11 → U 11	☐ • K 27 → O 26
☐ • P 12 → R 12	☐ • R 25 → Q 27
☐ • G 9 → I 9	☐ • P 24 → O 26
☐ • P 14 → V 14	☐ • K 27 → J 28
☐ • Y 14 → Z 14	☐ • Q 27 → M 28
☐ • U 15 → V 15	☐ • G 24 → D 27
☐ • Q 16 → T 16	☐ • V 22 → U 23
☐ • U 16 → W 16	☐ • H 22 → G 24
☐ • G 28 → J 28	☐ • V 22 → Z 20
☐ • S 21 → T 21	☐ • G 22 → D 27
☐ • U 24 → V 24	☐ • Y 8 → X 9
☐ • V 25 → W 25	☐ • Z 9 → Y 10
☐ • W 27 → X 27	☐ • Z 11 → Y 12
☐ • A 15 → A 19	☐ • A 19 → B 22
☐ • B 12 → B 13	☐ • B 25 → C 26
☐ • D 24 → D 27	☐ • C 21 → D 24
☐ • G 8 → G 9	☐ • A 22 → B 25
☐ • G 16 → G 18	☐ • H 15 → I 17
☐ • I 16 → I 17	☐ • H 8 → I 9
☐ • K 1 → K 4	☐ • I 14 → J 15
☐ • L 4 → L 6	☐ • S 18 → T 21
☐ • L 7 → L 8	☐ • U 24 → W 25
☐ • M 5 → M 6	☐ • W 27 → X 28
☐ • M 14 → M 17	☐ • S 21 → V 24
☐ • N 5 → N 6	☐ • V 25 → X 27
☐ • P 9 → P 12	☐ • X 9 → Y 10
☐ • U 11 → U 12	☐ • X 15 → Y 16
☐ • V 10 → V 12	☐ • O 17 → O 19
☐ • Y 10 → Y 14	☐ • N 12 → O 15
☐ • B 10 → A 11	☐ • M 17 → O 20
☐ • H 8 → K 6	☐ • O 15 → R 18
☐ • O 1 → M 5	☐ • L 16 → M 20
☐ • E 9 → D 10	☐ • M 13 → O 17
☐ • M 1 → L 4	☐ • A 11 → B 12
☐ • G 8 → E 9	☐ • D 8 → E 9
☐ • Q 1 → N 5	☐ • K 4 → L 6
☐ • J 8 → I 9	☐ • N 6 → O 7
☐ • B 13 → A 15	☐ • Q 1 → N 5
☐ • L 7 → J 8	☐ • T 10 → U 11
☐ • F 10 → I 9	☐ • L 8 → M 11
☐ • I 14 → H 15	☐ • U 12 → V 13
☐ • G 16 → F 17	☐ • O 7 → P 9
☐ • L 12 → I 14	☐ • V 12 → W 14
☐ • N 9 → M 11	☐ • P 10 → T 11
☐ • J 15 → I 16	☐ • M 7 → N 8
☐ • M 13 → L 16	☐ • O 13 → Q 16
	☐ • Q 7 → U 9
	☐ • R 12 → V 14

35

Symbols

After connecting a set of symbols, skip to another set of symbols and start your line again. Repeat for each set of symbols.

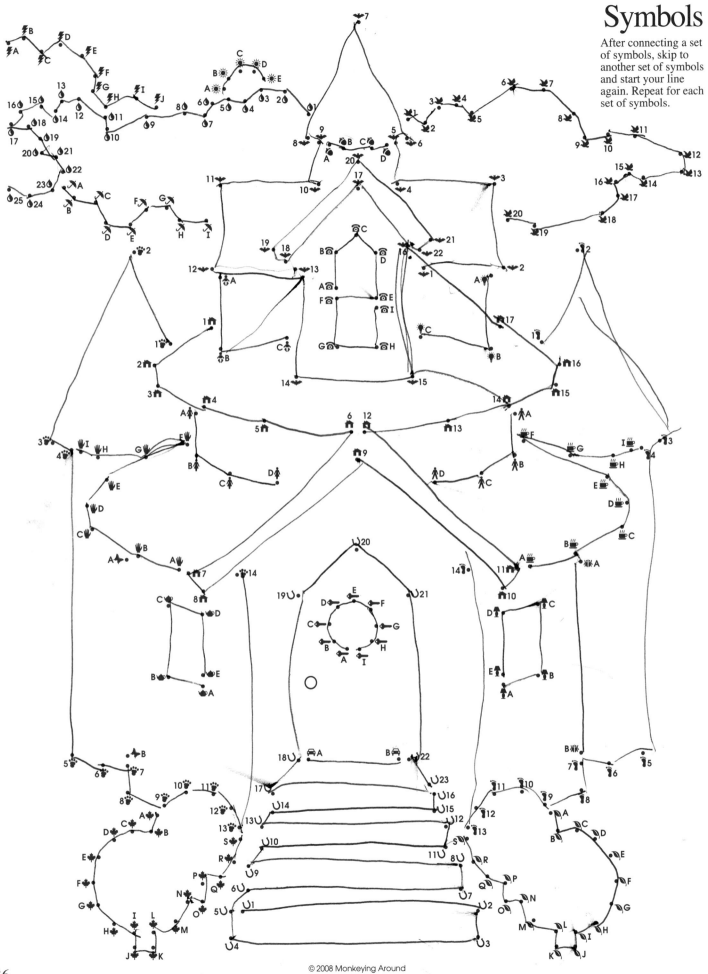

36

Stars

Stop at each star (★), then skip to the next number and start your line again.

End ★ 565

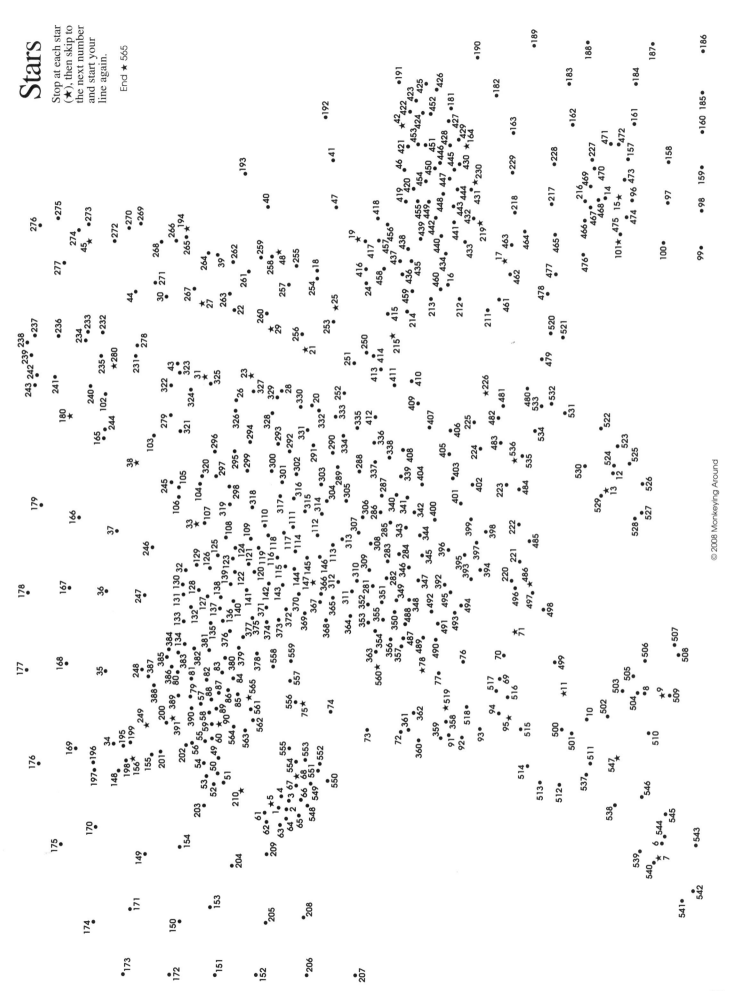

37

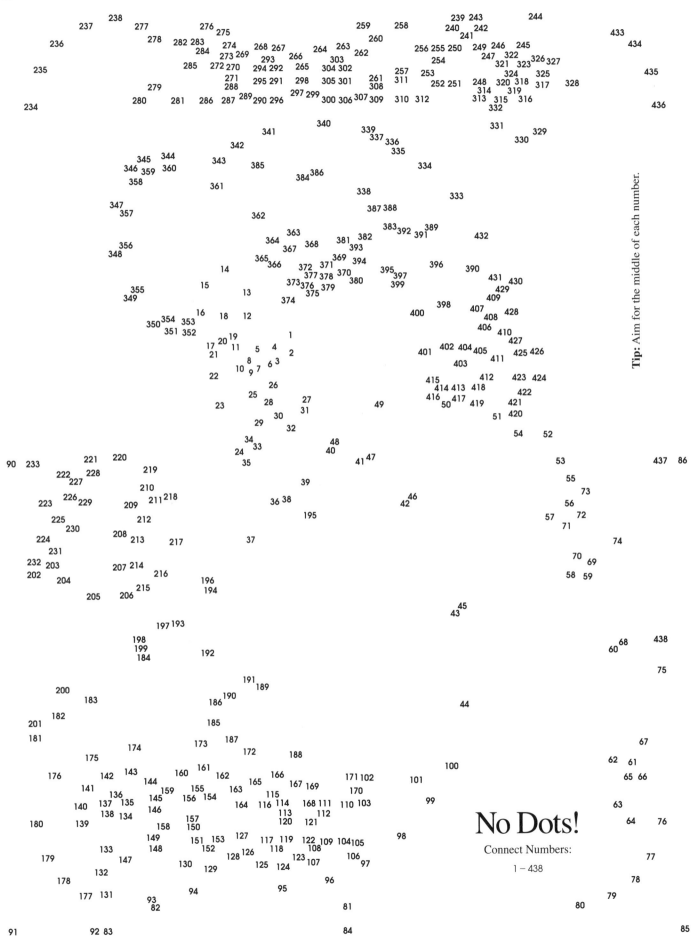

38

Alpha Dots

Start with the word "add", and connect all the words in alphabetical order, ending with the word "zoo".

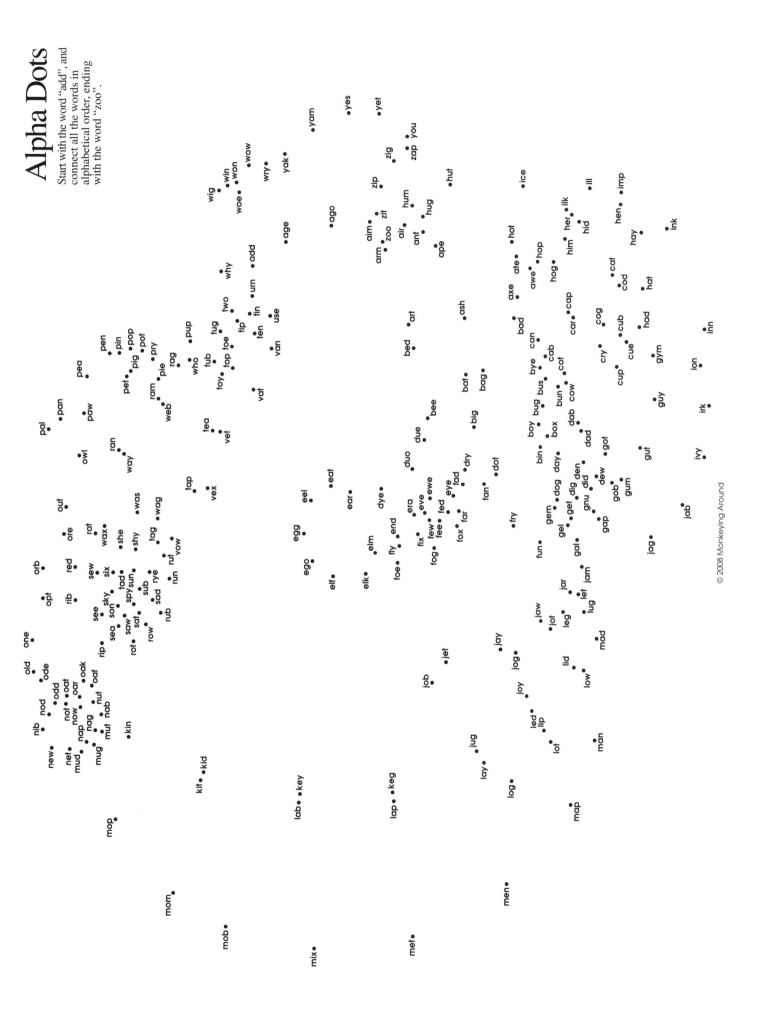

39

Sets

Stop your line after
completing each
set, then skip to the
next set and start
your line again.

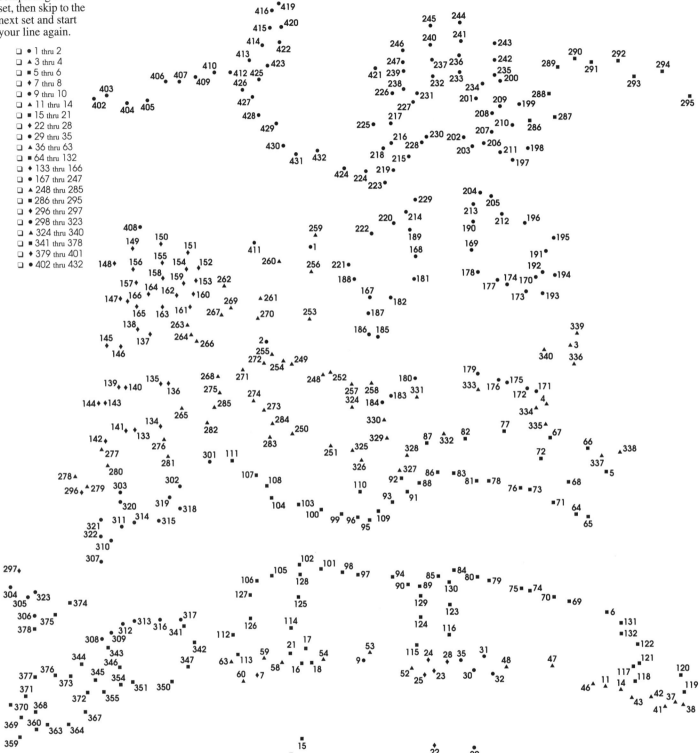

© 2008 Monkeying Around

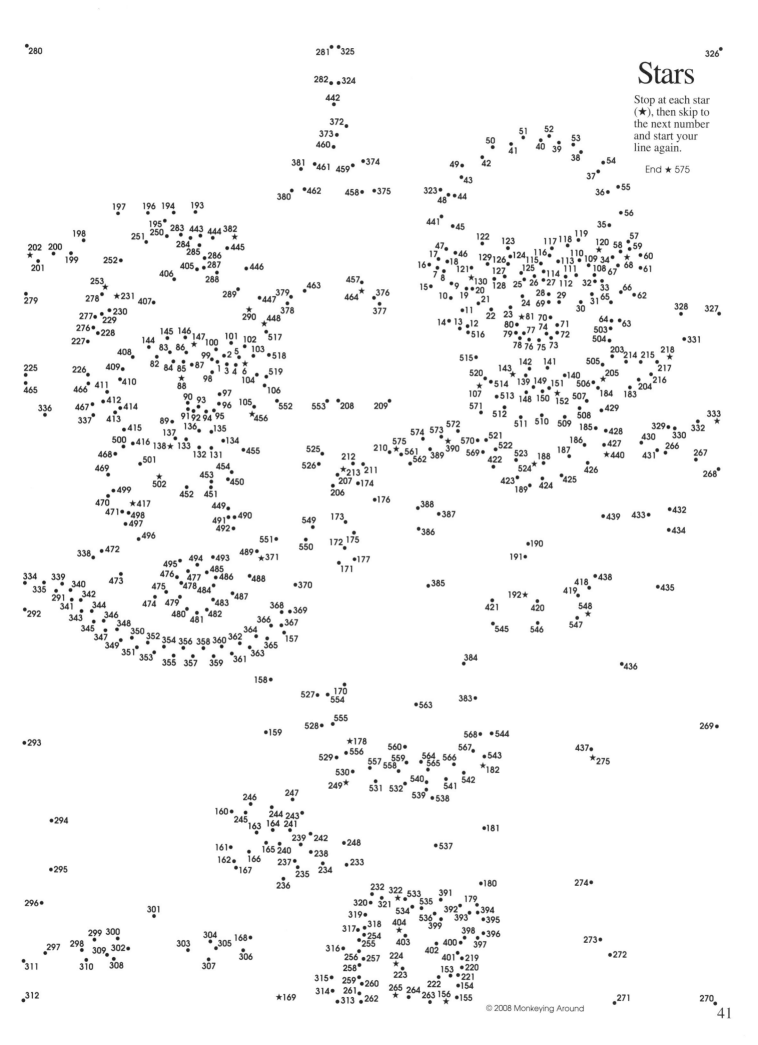

Stars

Stop at each star
(★), then skip to
the next number
and start your
line again.

End ★ 575

© 2008 Monkeying Around

41

☀ ➤ E ➤ NE x 2 ➤ E x 2 ➤ SE x 2 ➤ E ➤ SE x 5 ➤ S x 3 ➤ SW x 2 ➤ E ➤ NE ➤ N x 2 ➤ SE x 4 ➤ S ➤ SE ➤ S ➤ SE x 4 ➤ S ➤ SE x 2 = 🐦

🐦 ➤ S ➤ SE ➤ S x 7 ➤ NW ➤ N x 4 ➤ NW x 7 ➤ S ➤ SE x 6 ➤ S x 4 ➤ SE ➤ S x 3 ➤ SW x 2 ➤ S ➤ SW x 2 ➤ W ➤ SW x 2 ➤ W x 2 ➤ SW = 🦎

🦎 ➤ W x 2 ➤ NW x 10 ➤ NE x 5 ➤ E ➤ NE x 10 ➤ N x 2 ➤ NW ➤ S x 2 ➤ SW x 10 ➤ W ➤ SW x 5 ➤ W x 2 ➤ SW x 2 ➤ W x 2 ➤ SW ➤ W x 2 ➤ SW ➤ W x 2 = 🐢

🐢 ➤ NW x 4 ➤ N ➤ E x 3 ➤ NE ➤ E x 2 ➤ NE x 9 ➤ N ➤ SW x 9 ➤ W ➤ SW ➤ W ➤ SW ➤ W x 2 ➤ N x 2 ➤ NE ➤ S ➤ SE ➤ NE = ⚡

⚡ ➤ SE ➤ NE x 2 ➤ E ➤ SE ➤ NE ➤ N x 2 ➤ NE ➤ SE x 2 ➤ N x 2 ➤ NE ➤ SE x 2 ➤ N x 2 ➤ NE ➤ SE ➤ N ➤ W x 2 ➤ SW x 2 ➤ S = 🐇

🐇 ➤ SW x 3 ➤ S ➤ SW x 2 ➤ W ➤ SW ➤ NW ➤ SW ➤ N ➤ NE ➤ SE ➤ N ➤ NE ➤ SE x 2 ➤ N x 2 ➤ NE ➤ SE ➤ N ➤ NE x 2 = 🌲

🌲 ➤ N x 3 ➤ NE x 2 ➤ SE ➤ NE ➤ SE ➤ NE ➤ SE x 2 ➤ S x 4 ➤ E ➤ NE x 3 ➤ E ➤ NE ➤ E x 2 ➤ NE ➤ E ➤ NE ➤ E ➤ NE x 2 = 🦋

🦋 ➤ W x 7 ➤ NW ➤ W ➤ NW x 2 ➤ W x 4 ➤ SW x 2 ➤ NW x 2 ➤ SW x 3 ➤ NW ➤ N ➤ SW x 3 ➤ NW ➤ N x 2 ➤ SW x 3 ➤ NW ➤ N x 2 ➤ SW x 2 ➤ NW = 💧

💧 ➤ N x 2 ➤ SE ➤ E ➤ SE x 2 ➤ E ➤ SE ➤ E x 2 ➤ SE ➤ E x 2 ➤ NE ➤ SE x 6 ➤ SE x 2 ➤ E ➤ SE x 2 ➤ E x 5 ➤ NW ➤ W x 3 ➤ NW = 🍄

🍄 ➤ E ➤ NW ➤ W ➤ NW ➤ W ➤ NW ➤ W x 3 ➤ NW ➤ W x 3 ➤ NW x 2 ➤ W ➤ NW ➤ W ➤ NW x 3 ➤ N ➤ NE ➤ E ➤ NE = 🐾

🐾 ➤ E ➤ NE x 2 ➤ NW ➤ W ➤ SW ➤ W ➤ SW x 3 ➤ S ➤ SW ➤ NW ➤ N ➤ NE x 6 ➤ E ➤ NE x 2 ➤ E x 3 ➤ SE ➤ E x 2 ➤ NE = 🐻

🐻 ➤ E x 2 ➤ SW ➤ W ➤ SW ➤ W x 3 ➤ SW ➤ S ➤ NE x 2 ➤ E x 2 ➤ SE ➤ E x 2 ➤ SE ➤ E ➤ NE x 3 ➤ E x 2 ➤ SE x 4 ➤ SW ➤ S x 2 = ▲

▲ ➤ SW ➤ W x 2 ➤ NW x 3 ➤ E ➤ SE ➤ E ➤ NE ➤ N ➤ NE ➤ NW x 3 ➤ W ➤ SW x 4 ➤ E ➤ NE x 2 ➤ E ➤ SE ➤ SW x 2 ➤ W ➤ NE x 2 = 🌙

Compass

Start at the sun (☀), and follow the compass directions to the next dot in the sequence. Each line of instructions will lead you to a symbol, to help keep you on track.

Stars

Stop at each star (★), then skip to the next number and start your line again.

End ★ 692

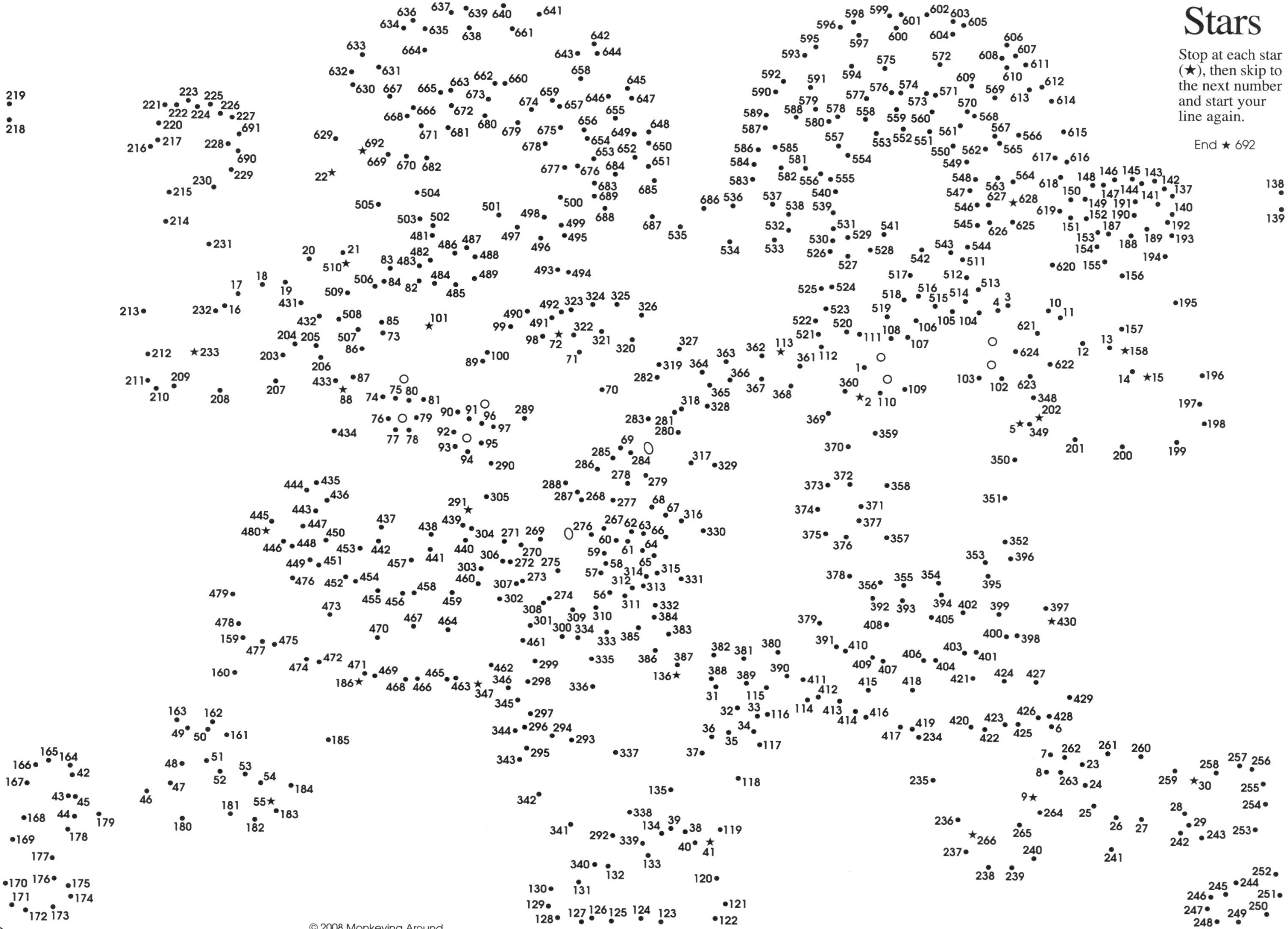

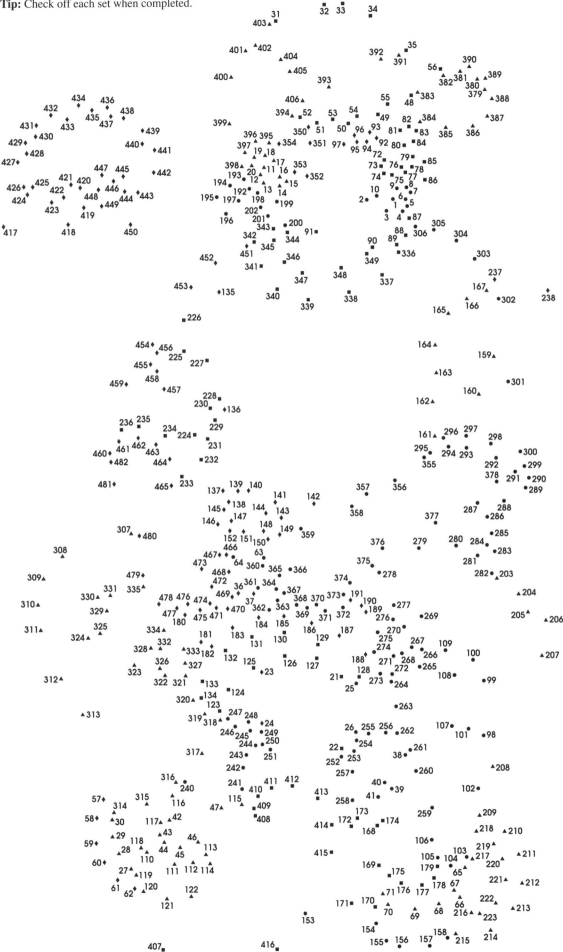

Sets

Stop your line after completing each set, then skip to the next set and start your line again.

- ● 1 thru 10
- ▲ 11 thru 20
- ■ 21 thru 22
- ◆ 23 thru 24
- ● 25 thru 26
- ▲ 27 thru 30
- ■ 31 thru 35
- ◆ 36 thru 37
- ● 38 thru 41
- ▲ 42 thru 47
- ■ 48 thru 56
- ◆ 57 thru 62
- ● 63 thru 64
- ▲ 65 thru 71
- ■ 72 thru 91
- ◆ 92 thru 97
- ● 98 thru 109
- ▲ 110 thru 122
- ■ 123 thru 134
- ◆ 135 thru 152
- ● 153 thru 158
- ▲ 159 thru 167
- ■ 168 thru 179
- ◆ 180 thru 191
- ● 192 thru 202
- ▲ 203 thru 223
- ■ 224 thru 236
- ◆ 237 thru 239
- ● 240 thru 306
- ▲ 307 thru 335
- ■ 336 thru 349
- ◆ 350 thru 354
- ● 355 thru 378
- ▲ 379 thru 406
- ■ 407 thru 416
- ◆ 417 thru 482

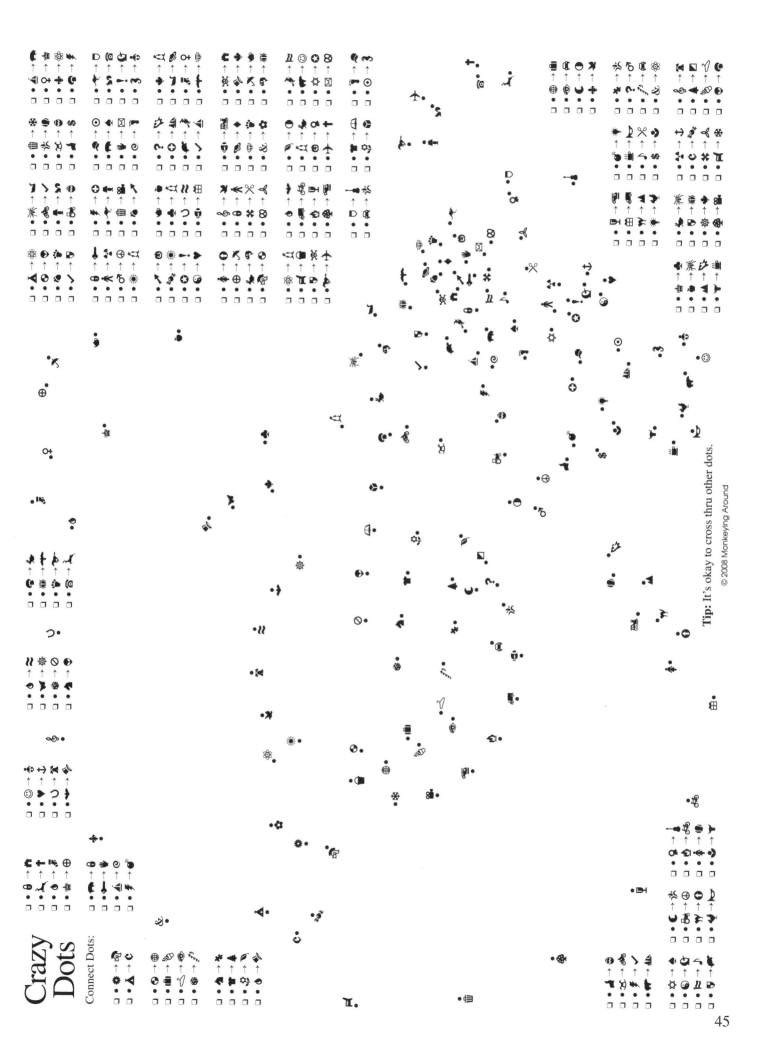

Crazy Dots

Connect Dots:

Tip: It's okay to cross thru other dots.

© 2008 Monkeying Around

45

Arrows

Start at circled arrow. Move pen in the direction circled arrow points, to the middle of the next arrow. Follow the direction each arrow points. End at circled dot.

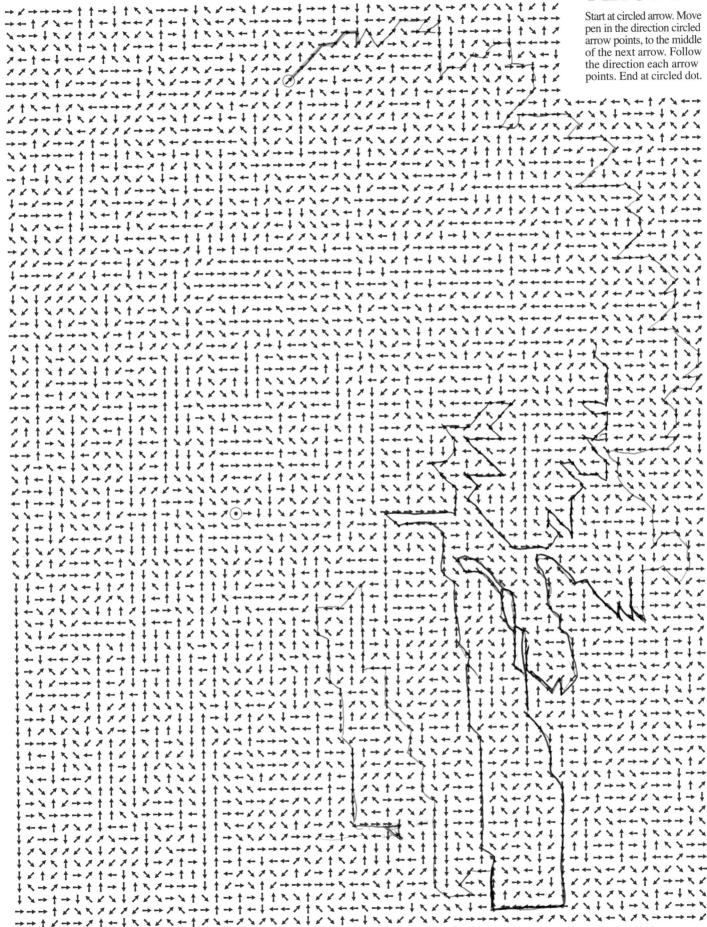

Stars

Stop at each star (★), then skip to the next number and start your line again.

End ★ 668

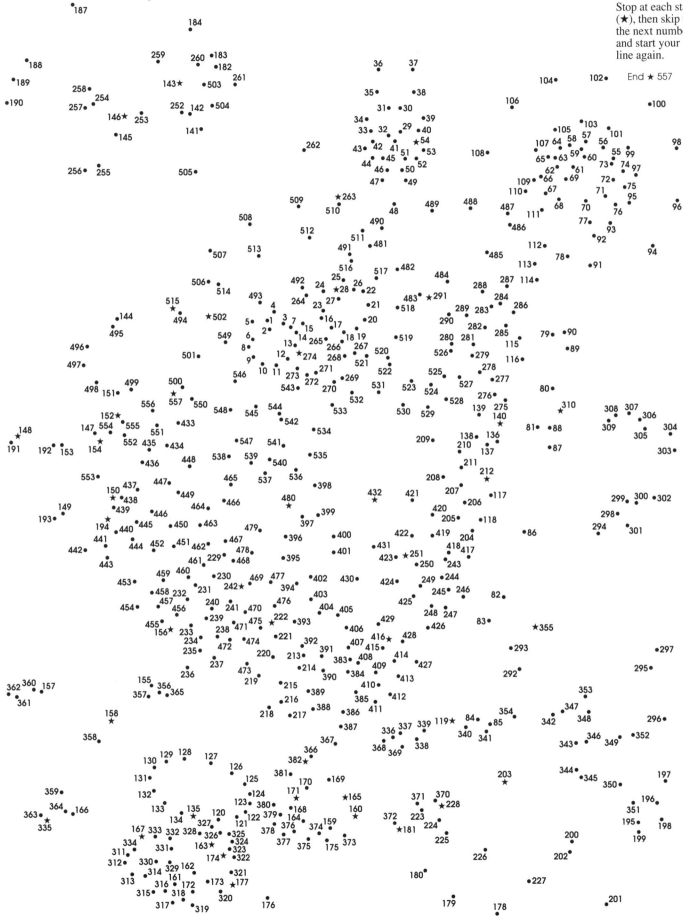

Stars

Stop at each star (★), then skip to the next number and start your line again.

End ★ 557